Quick and Clever Fleece

Quick and Clever Fleece

20 Easy-Sew Projects

Lynne Farris

Creative Publishing international

Chanhassen, MN

Creative Publishing
international

Copyright 2006
Creative Publishing international
18705 Lake Drive East
Chanhassen, Minnesota 55317
1-800-328-3895
www.creativepub.com
All rights reserved

President/CEO: Ken Fund
Executive Editor: Alison Brown Cerier
Executive Managing Editor: Barbara Harold
Senior Editor: Linda Neubauer
Photo Stylist: Joanne Wawra
Creative Director: Brad Springer
Photo Art Director: Tim Himsel
Photographers: Steve Galvin, John Haglof, Joel Schnell
Illustrator: M. Deborah Pierce
Production Manager: Laura Hokkanen
Cover and Book Design: Brian Donahue / bedesign, inc.

Library of Congress Cataloging-in-Publication Data

Farris, Lynne.
  Quick & clever fleece : 20 easy-sew fashions / Lynne Farris.
    p. cm.
ISBN-13: 978-1-58923-258-7 (soft cover)
  ISBN-10: 1-58923-258-5 (soft cover)
  1. Machine sewing. 2. Polyester fibers. I. Title: Quick and
clever fleece. II. Title.
  TT713.F367 2006
  646'.11--dc22   2006002492

Printed in Singapore
10 9 8 7 6 5 4 3 2 1

Acknowledgments
For almost twenty years I have shared an extraordinary creative
collaboration with my friend Mary Woodall, in whose skillful
hands even my wackiest fabric ideas, sketched out loosely on a
scrap of paper, have been magically transformed into glorious
reality. Her talent, curiosity, tenacity, enthusiasm, and sense of
humor are at the heart of all these projects. Thanks, Mary.

Special thanks to Lambert Greene for numerous late-night runs
to the airport FedEx drop-off, and to Laylee Asgari who served as
our studio model, trend adviser, and all-around fashionista.
Thanks to the company June Tailor, Inc., for providing special
rulers and tools for working with fleece.

Contents

Fresh Fleece

Quick and Clever Fleece is a new approach to this colorful, cozy, stylish, wildly popular fabric. These original projects feature unique techniques, new fleece products, and clever embellishments.

I've designed fleece projects for you, your home, and everybody on your gift list. There are toys and nap quilts for preschoolers, fashion accessories for tweens or teens, contemporary home décor accents, hostess gifts, some great projects to make for the men in your life, and items to pamper yourself—scarves, home spa accessories, an arty tote, and more.

"Fleece" is the generic name for a group of lofty, stretchy fabrics made of synthetic fibers. Of all the specialty fabrics, it is the best seller. Many people associate fleece with the beefy kinds used in coats and warm hats, but fleece is not just for winter anymore. There are all kinds of fleece in fabric stores now—very thin, super-thick, two-sided, textured, furry, and more. These new fleece fabrics are perfect for fashion, home décor, and crafts. The colors have evolved, too. You can now find fashion colors and patterns as well as basic colors and outdoorsy patterns.

No matter how much sewing you've done (or not done), you're going to love sewing with fleece. Raw edges won't fray, even when washed, which makes fleece perfect for fringes, raw-edge appliqué, and exposed seams as a design element. The edges of fleece can be easily cut into scallops and other decorative lines. Because fleece is stretchy but sturdy, matching seams and sewing around curves is a breeze. The loft of the fabric covers a multitude of sewing sins, so your projects will look professional and neat with a minimum of fuss. Fleece is washable and durable, too. You'll be hooked on sewing with fleece in no time.

Each project has step-by-step instructions, photographs, and patterns. The patterns that must be enlarged are printed on a grid so you can enlarge them on a copy machine or redraw them on ½" (1.3 cm) graph paper. A basics section covers special techniques and tips for working with fleece—please read it before starting on a project.

I hope you will have as much fun making these projects as we have had presenting them to you.

Lynne Farris

The Author

Lynne Farris is a fabric artist and frequent guest on HGTV. Her designs have been featured in magazines including *Family Circle*, *Sew News*, and *McCalls*. She is the author of *Baby Crafts* and *Sewing Fun Stuff: Soft Sculpture Shortcuts* and owner of Lynne Farris Gallery in Atlanta, Georgia, where many of her textile works are on display. To learn more about Lynne, visit her website, www.lynnefarrisdesigns.com.

Sewing with Fleece

These basics and tips will make sewing with fleece easier and more successful.

The Basics

Fleece is the general term for a category of lofty knitted fabrics made from synthetic fiber. Available in a variety of weights, textures, colors, and prints, fleece is washable and machine dryable. It doesn't shrink or fade and is incredibly easy to sew, even for beginners. It usually comes in fairly wide widths. It is inexpensive compared to other knitted fabrics.

Stretch

While all fleeces stretch, the amount varies a lot. It's important to know what you are dealing with before you launch into a project, especially a garment. Most project instructions recommend a certain type or weight of fleece if it will make a difference in the success of the project. When you're buying fleece, test it by stretching from selvage to selvage (on the crosswise grain) to see how much stretch is knitted in. Some of the furry fleeces have very little stretch, while others behave like a swimsuit fabric with stretch in all directions.

Right and Wrong Sides

Although some fleece fabrics have an obvious right and wrong, many look the same on both sides—until you get them sewn together wrong, that is. Here's how to tell right from wrong (at least with fleece). Stretch the cut edge of the fleece in the crosswise direction (usually the direction of greatest stretch). It will curl toward the wrong side. Once you determine the right and wrong sides, mark each piece of your fabric carefully to be sure that you are consistent throughout the project with right and wrong sides.

Texture and Weight

A trip to the fabric store will reveal a huge variety of traditional and new fleeces. Weights range from very thin to extra thick. Double-sided fleece is made of two fleece layers in contrasting colors, bonded together to form a very cuddly warm and almost weather-proof fabric. Some very interesting fleeces feature a sculpted surface like ribbed or waffle.

Some projects in the book use the very silky, furry fleece that has become very popular. While technically not a fleece, this fabric is similar to and compatible with fleece.

Marking Fabric

Marking directly on the fabric is recommended in several projects for which you actually sew the seam, then cut out beyond your stitching line. In this case, you can use an air soluble marker or chalk marker; experiment on a scrap to see what works better on the particular fabric.

You will find that many of the pattern templates in the pattern section call for tracing around the template, then sewing along the traced line before cutting out. It's very important to read all instructions before beginning to cut and to make sure that you accurately trace and cut each pattern.

Cutting Fleece

Fleece is easy to cut, especially with a rotary cutter, straightedge, and cutting mat. Since the raw edges don't fray, you can use the cut edges to add a decorative touch by cutting with a pinking blade or pinking shears.

Another creative way to cut fleece is to make "faux chenille," as shown in the Crazy Kaleidoscope Pillow. Two layers of fleece are sewn together with parallel rows of stitching. The top layer is then slit between the rows of stitching to reveal the color below.

Needles and Thread

Start with a fresh ballpoint needle at the beginning of each project. For most of the projects, a size 80/12 needle is appropriate. When you must sew through several heavy layers, switch to a size 90/14 needle. Set the stitch length around 3 or 3.5 mm. Since there are many kinds of fleece, it's a good idea to stitch a little on a scrap before you start sewing the project. If you find that your machine is skipping stitches, loosen the tension slightly and try it again. If you'll be using decorative or zigzag stitches, experiment with some of those to see how they look on your particular fleece.

Choose good quality long staple polyester thread in a matching or slightly darker color than the fabric you are sewing.

Stabilizers and Stiffeners

A temporary spray adhesive is very useful for adhering together layers that will be sewn. It will also keep appliqués from slipping and will hold batting in place underneath the fabric surface. Tear-away stabilizer works well for stitching appliqués—often I simply use paper as the stabilizer. Some projects call for extra-stiff interfacing such as Timtex. This material adds stability, weight, and sturdiness to the project.

Laundering

Fleece is easy to launder using a simple laundry detergent—no fabric softeners, either liquid or sheet. Machine wash, following your machine's guidelines for temperature, and dry on medium heat in your dryer for best results. The good news is, ironing is not recommended. If you must, use a warm iron with steam and hold it above the surface, not touching the fabric with the iron, then smoothing the fabric with your fingers. Seam allowances are usually narrow and don't need to be spread apart.

Add just the right air of frivolity to a sweater or jacket with this feather-light boa. You can make a relatively sedate boa of three

Loopy Boa

coordinating colors, or raid your fleece scraps for a boa of many colors. (The scraps need to be large enough that you can cut strips ½" (1.3 cm) wide and at least 15" (38 cm) long in the direction of greatest stretch.) Once the boa is together, a quick pluck on each loop fluffs it out. Make one for your inner fashionista.

MATERIALS

- 9" × 60" (23 × 152.5 cm) tear-away stabilizer (can be pieced together)
- Tape, optional
- Yardstick (meterstick) or tape measure
- Fabric marking pen or pencil
- ¼ yd. (0.25 m) each of three coordinating, very stretchy, fleeces (or an equal amount of scraps in various colors and patterns)
- Rotary cutter, cutting mat, and straightedge
- Matching thread

1. Cut pieces of tear-away stabilizer 9" (23 cm) wide, and tape or pin them together to a length of 60" (152.5 cm).

2. Mark a line down the center of the stabilizer strip. Then mark lines 3" (7.5 cm) to the left and right of the center line.

3. Trim away the selvages of the fleece. Fold the fleece in half lengthwise, aligning the cut edges. Then fold in half lengthwise again, aligning the fold to the cut edges. Cut the fleece crosswise into ½" (1.3 cm) strips, using a rotary cutter, cutting mat, and straightedge.

4. Set the sewing machine for a long straight triple stitch (stretch stitch) or narrow, short zigzag. Place the end of one fleece strip over the center line of the stabilizer, and stitch it down. Leaving the presser foot down, fold the fleece strip back and forth at the outer lines, edges touching, and continue stitching down the center. When one strip ends, begin another, and continue to the end of the stabilizer.

5. Repeat step 4 with a second layer of fleece strips, stitching over the first layer. Then add a third layer of loops.

6. Center a fleece strip over the previous stitching lines, and stitch through all layers.

7. Carefully tear away the stabilizer. Pull and release each loop to stretch and curl the boa. Fluff the boa in the dryer to remove extra lint.

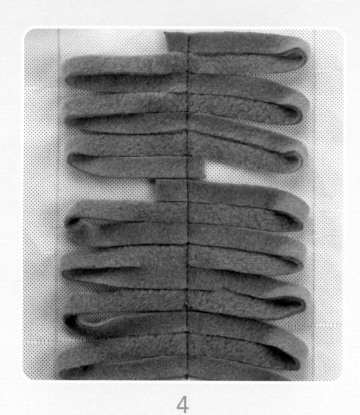

4

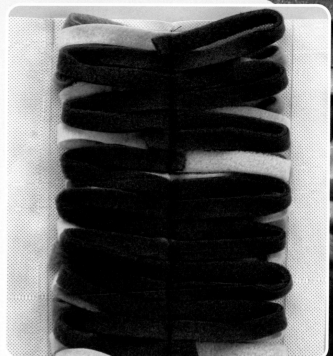

5

6

Pamper a fine sweater or silk blouse by storing it on a thickly padded, luxury hanger. This is an

Rosebud Padded Hangers

haute couture hanger that will dress up your closet. Embellished with a dimensional sculpted rosebud and tiny button details, this hanger is soft and feminine.

MATERIALS

- Copy machine or graph paper for enlarging pattern
- ⅝ yd. (0.6 m) medium-weight fleece
- Temporary spray adhesive, such as Sulky KK2000
- Fabric marking pen or pencil
- Medium-weight batting, about 22" × 30" (56 × 76 cm)
- Open-toe embroidery foot
- Matching thread
- Plastic hanger
- Six ½" (1.3 cm) buttons
- Glue gun and glue sticks
- 4" × 7" (10 × 18 cm) fleece scrap for leaves
- 6" × 9" (15 × 23 cm) fleece scrap for rosebud
- Pinking shears or pinking rotary cutter

1. Enlarge the pattern on page 95, and cut it out.

2. Cut the fleece in half lengthwise. Adhere the pattern to the wrong side of one piece of fleece, using temporary adhesive spray. Trace the pattern outline onto the fleece, using a fabric marking pen or marker. Transfer all markings. Remove the pattern.

3. Pin the two pieces of fleece, right sides together, with the marked pattern facing up. Spray the batting lightly with temporary adhesive, and layer the fleece over the batting.

4. Attach an open-toe embroidery foot to the sewing machine. Stitch the layers together along the traced stitching lines of the scallop edges and square center hook opening. Pivot at the corners, leaving the needle down in the fabric.

5. Cut out the hanger cover, cutting close to the stitched edges and along the marked cutting lines of the edges that are not stitched. Clip into the corners up to, but not through, the stitching lines.

6. Turn the hanger cover right side out. Fold the cover in half, aligning the center back seam allowances. Stitch the center back seam. Trim the seam allowances diagonally at the lower edge. Zigzag the two seam allowances of each edge together to neaten.

7. Refold the hanger cover, aligning the seam allowances on the sides. Stitch the side seams. Zigzag the two seam allowances of each edge together to neaten.

8. Turn the cover right side out. Insert the hanger. Mark button placement and sew on buttons through all layers. Use temporary adhesive to hold buttons in place for accurate placement.

9. Trace the template for the hook cover on page 96, and cut it out. Cut out a hook cover from a scrap of the leftover fleece. Fold the cover in half, right sides together, and sew a ¼" (6 mm) seam on the long edge and point. Turn the hook cover right side out, and slip it onto the hook so the "tail" extends onto the hanger. Secure the tail to the hanger with hot glue.

10. Trace the template for the rosebud on page 96, and cut it out. Fold the rosebud fleece in half lengthwise, wrong sides together, and align the template to the fold. Trace the template edge using a fabric marking pen or pencil. Stitch along the traced outline. Cut out the rosebud, using pinking shears or a pinking rotary cutter.

11. Trace the leaf template on page 96, and cut it out. Fold the leaf fleece in half lengthwise, wrong sides together, and center the template over the layers. Trace the template edge using a fabric marking pen or pencil. Stitch along the traced outline and down the center. Cut out the leaves, using pinking shears or a pinking rotary cutter. Pinch the sides together slightly off-center, and secure with hot glue to form a pair of leaves.

12. Roll the rosebud, starting very tightly at one end and getting gradually looser. Secure the lower edge with drops of hot glue as you roll. Glue the rosebud between the leaves. Glue the rosebud and leaves below the hanger hook.

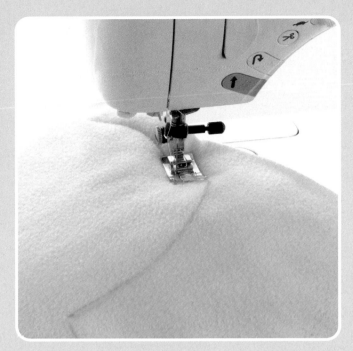

4

5

12

Even a beginner can make this
pair of stylish and comfy slippers
with professional-looking binding.

Lady Slippers

We've dressed them up with large
bows made in quite a clever way
from a coordinating print fleece.

MATERIALS

- Copy machine or graph paper for enlarging patterns
- ⅓ yd. (0.32 m) fleece
- Ruler
- Temporary spray adhesive, such as Sulky KK2000
- 12" (30.5 cm) square stiff interfacing, such as Timtex
- 12" (30.5 cm) square flannel-backed non-skid fabric
- Fabric marking pen or pencil
- Matching thread
- ¼ yd. (0.25 m) fleece for bows
- Hand-sewing needle

1. Enlarge the patterns on page 97, and cut them out. Cut a 12" (30.5 cm) square of fleece. Apply spray adhesive to one side of the stiff interfacing, following the manufacturer's directions. Place the fleece wrong side down on the interfacing and smooth to adhere. Turn the interfacing over, apply adhesive to the other side, and adhere the wrong side of the nonskid fabric. Enlarge the sole pattern twice onto the fabric sandwich and cut it out carefully along the traced lines.

2. To make the upper slippers, start by folding the remaining fleece in half, right sides together. Trace the upper slipper pattern on page 98 and trace it twice onto the double thickness of fleece. Cut them out. Sew the two layers together along the lower curved edge using ¼" (6 mm) seam allowance. Turn them right side out.

3. Pin an upper slipper to the fabric side of a sole, matching the points at the toes. Sew around the outer edges using ¼" (6 mm) seam allowance. Trim evenly. Repeat for the other slipper.

4. To make the binding, cut two fleece strips 2½" (6.5 cm) wide and as long as the outside edge of the sole plus 2" (5 cm). Beginning at the lower side edge of the slipper, align the edge of the binding with the edge of the sole. Tugging the binding slightly, stitch ¼" (6 mm) seam around the slipper, overlapping the beginning of the binding by about 1½" (3.8 cm). Trim the seam allowances evenly.

5. Wrap the binding over the seam allowance to the underside of the slipper. Working from the top of the slipper, stitch in the ditch of the seam to secure the wrapped binding to the underside of the sole. Trim close to the stitching line.

6. To make the bows, trace the bow pattern onto a double thickness of fleece, matching the arrow with the direction of greatest stretch. Sew on the traced lines. Cut out the bows, leaving about ¼" (6 mm) seam allowance.

7. Cut a 1" (2.5 cm) slit in the center of the bow through one layer. Turn the bow right side out. Tie a knot in the center of the bow, enclosing the slit. Pull the ends to shape the knot and bow. Repeat for the second bow. Hand-stitch the bows onto the upper slippers.

1

3

4

7

Fleece works remarkably well for creating soft-sculpture adorn-ments like this lovely cluster of

Calla Lily Adornment

calla lilies. Use them to adorn the collar of a bathrobe or the toes of your new fleece slippers. Add a lily cluster to any hand-made gift to make it even more special.

MATERIALS

- Cardstock
- ⅛ yd. (0.15 m) each of white, green, and yellow fleece
- Ruler
- Fabric marking pen or pencil
- Matching thread
- Hand-sewing needle
- Pin backing, optional
- Computer with word processing software and printer
- Printable fabric sheet for labels, such as Printed Treasures™

1. Trace the flower, stamen, and leaf patterns (page 99) onto cardstock and cut them out carefully.

2. Cut two pieces of white fleece, 10" × 4" (25.5 × 10 cm); two pieces of green fleece, 3" × 8" (7.5 × 20.5 cm); and two pieces of yellow fleece, 3" × 4" (7.5 × 10 cm). Layer each set of fabrics right sides together.

3. Trace the flower pattern three times onto the top layer of white fleece, leaving at least ½" (1.3 cm) space between them. Trace the stamen pattern onto the top layer of yellow fleece. Trace the leaf pattern onto the top layer of green fleece. Stitch on the marked lines on all the pieces. Leave the bottom straight edge of the stamens open.

4. Cut out the petals, stamens, and leaves, leaving ¼" (6 mm) seam allowances all around. Turn the stamens right side out. Then cut across the bottom of the stamens, as indicated on the pattern. Slit the petals through one thickness near the lower edge, and turn them right side out through the slit. Slit the leaf through one thickness in the center and turn it right side out through the slit.

5. Turn in the raw edges of the stamens and hand-stitch them closed. Place a stamen in the center of a petal, near the lower edge, and hand-stitch it in place. Pinch together the lower edges of the petal over the stamen and hand-stitch to shape the flower. Repeat with the other two flowers.

6. Roll the outer edges of the leaf together at the center, encasing the slit, and stitch them together to shape the leaves.

7. Using the photo on page 23 as a guide, arrange the flowers over the leaves and hand-stitch them in place. Stitch the cluster to the item you want to adorn, or stitch a pin backing onto the back of the leaves to make it removable.

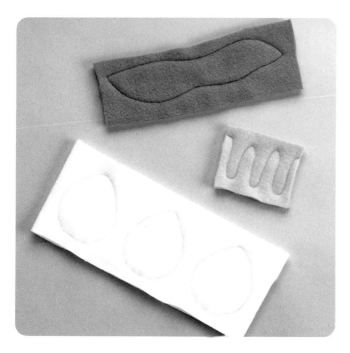

3

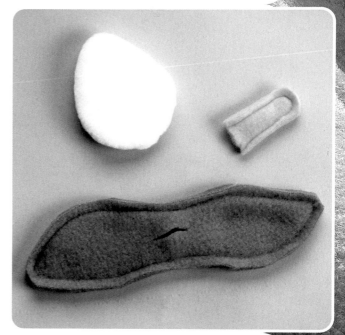

4

6

This scarf has an understated elegance. No one will suspect that it's simply a strip of ordinary

Pintucked Scarf

fleece that has been embellished with easy pintuck double-needle stitching to create the lavish sculpted lattice pattern. Finished at both ends with a simple fringe, the scarf can be made in just a few hours, thanks to some help from a couple of really useful special rulers.

MATERIALS

- ⅓ yd. (0.32 m) medium-weight or lightweight fleece
- Yardstick (meterstick) or tape measure
- Fabric marking pen or pencil
- June Tailor® Fancy Fleece™ cutting ruler
- Rotary cutter, cutting mat, and straightedge
- Double needle for stretch fabrics
- Two spools of matching thread
- June Tailor® Fringe Cut™ ruler

1. Cut a 10" (25.5 cm) strip across the full width of the fleece. Trim off the selvages at the ends. Mark the center point on both long edges.

2. Align the guideline on the Fancy Fleece cutting ruler to the cut edge of the fabric, so the wave edge is inward. Beginning 5" (12.7 cm) from one end, trace the wave pattern onto the fleece, using a fabric marking pen or pencil. Carefully match and repeat the wave pattern as needed, ending 5" (12.7 cm) from the other end. Repeat along the opposite long edge so the wavy lines mirror each other.

3. Mark the centers of the high and low points of each wave. Connect the points to create a lattice pattern between the wavy lines. Mark a line straight across each end.

4. Thread the sewing machine for double-needle stitching. Beginning at one end, sew across the end, following the marked lines, and continue following the wavy pattern all the way around the outer edges. Do not remove the scarf from the machine.

5. Continue double-needle stitching along the marked lattice lines. When you reach the opposite end, sew across the end right next to the first pintuck, and continue stitching from point to point on the remaining lattice lines back to the end where you started. Stitch a second line across the end. Backstitch carefully and trim any loose thread ends from the underside.

6. To create fringe, draw a line ½" (1.3 cm) from the stitching on each end of the scarf. Align a guideline of the Fringe Cut ruler to the marked line on the scarf, and cut the fringe with a rotary cutter. Repeat on the other end.

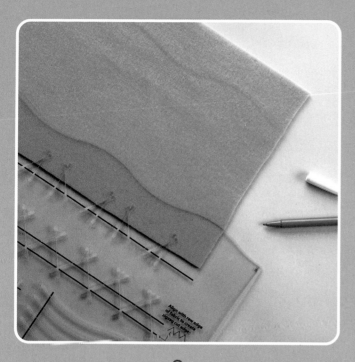

2

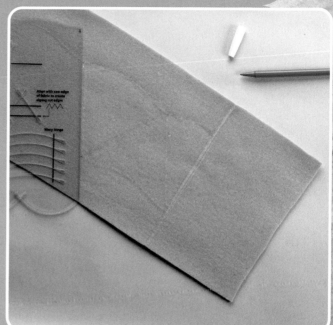

3

6

These pedicure booties are a perfect gift for pampering your mom, friend, sister, or yourself. The removable inner booties are filled with rice and scented with

Home Spa Booties

lavender buds. A few seconds in the microwave will warm them up for a comforting and fragrant spa experience. For the full treatment, slather your feet with a soothing lotion, put on a pair of thin cotton socks, then slide into the toasty booties. Put your feet up and close your eyes for twenty minutes while the heat and the lotion do their good work.

MATERIALS

- Copy machine or graph paper for enlarging pattern
- 1 yd. (0.92 m) medium-weight fleece (allow more for matching plaid)
- ½ yd. (0.5 m) coordinating fleece for bootie covers
- Fabric marking pen or pencil
- Matching thread
- Funnel
- Two pounds (900 g) raw uncooked rice
- 2 oz. (57 g) lavender buds, optional, mixed well with rice

1. Enlarge the bootie and sole patterns on pages 101 and 102, and cut them out. Arrange the bootie fabric in a double layer. Trace and cut out four double bootie sections and two double sole sections. Transfer the pattern markings to the fabric.

2. Pin each double-layer bootie section together. Stitch along the marked channel lines.

3. Stitch two sections together from the top to the heel and from the top to the toe, using a ¼" (6 mm) seam allowance. Leave openings between the dots (arrows). Repeat for the other bootie. Stitch around the top of each bootie, ¼" (6 mm) from the edge.

4. Stitch two sole pieces, wrong sides together, leaving an opening between the dots (arrow) on one side.

5. Stitch a sole to a bootie, matching at the heel and toe, and leaving an opening between the dots on both sides. One side will have an opening in the sole and the side channel for filling; the other side will have an opening only in the side channel.

6. Insert the funnel into each sole and fill with about one cup (200 g) of the rice/lavender mixture. Pin closed.

7. Insert the funnel into each channel and fill with about ⅓ cup (66 g) of the rice mixture. Pin closed. Stitch all the openings closed.

8. To make the bootie covers, fold the outer edges of the coordinating fabric to the center. Place the pattern heel seam lines on the folds. Cut two bootie covers and two bootie cover soles.

9. Stitch the center front seams, right sides together. Pin the soles to the bootie covers, right sides together, and stitch. Turn the bootie covers right side out.

10. To use, heat the inner booties in the microwave on high for 10 to 30 seconds. Slip the inner booties into the covers. Wear them over socks. The outer booties can be laundered normally. The inner booties should only be surface washed with a damp cloth.

3

4

6

7

Here's a great-looking shawl with clever two-way pockets that can open from the top or the side.

Confetti Shawl

This project showcases a colorful new fleece technique—adapted from traditional ribbon weaving—that emphasizes pattern and texture while adding several layers of warmth to the pocket areas. Use up your scraps while you learn a new technique and create a cozy gift.

MATERIALS

- 1 yd. (0.92 m) medium-weight solid-color fleece
- Yardstick (meterstick) or tape measure
- ⅔ yd. (0.63 m) total additional fleece in a variety of colors and patterns
- Pinking rotary cutter and cutting mat, optional
- Pinking shears
- Thread to match background color

1. Cut a full crosswise strip of fleece, 26" (66 cm) wide, for the shawl. Cut two 13" × 9" (33 cm × 23 cm) pieces for the pockets.

2. Cut twelve 1½" × 13" (3.8 × 33 cm) strips and fourteen 1½" × 9" (3.8 × 23 cm) strips of the various colored and patterned fleeces, using pinking shears or a pinking rotary cutter.

3. Arrange six of the longer strips side by side on each pocket piece, and pin them in place. In the opposite direction, weave seven of the shorter strips in and out of the pinned strips. Move pins as necessary.

4. Set sewing machine for a darning stitch or a small decorative pattern such as a starburst and stitch in the center of each square formed by the woven strips. Stitch continuously, moving from one square to another.

5. Clip all threads close to the stitching on the front and back of each pocket piece. Use pinking shears to cut through the woven strips in both directions, creating small, layered squares. Be careful not to cut the background piece.

6. Place the pocket squares on two opposite corners of the shawl, matching the outer edges and aligning the short inner edges of the pockets to the center of the shawl. Pin. Stitch through both layers close to all edges of the pockets. Push the layered squares out of the way as necessary. Leave an 8" (20.5 cm) opening in the center of the inner long edge.

7. Fold the shawl in half, wrong sides together, and pin. Stitch across the ends, keeping the layered squares free. Stitch the long shawl edges together, leaving a centered 6" (15 cm) opening in the side of each pocket.

8. To fluff out the confetti, grasp each pair of small squares and twist and pull diagonally to stretch and curl the fleece.

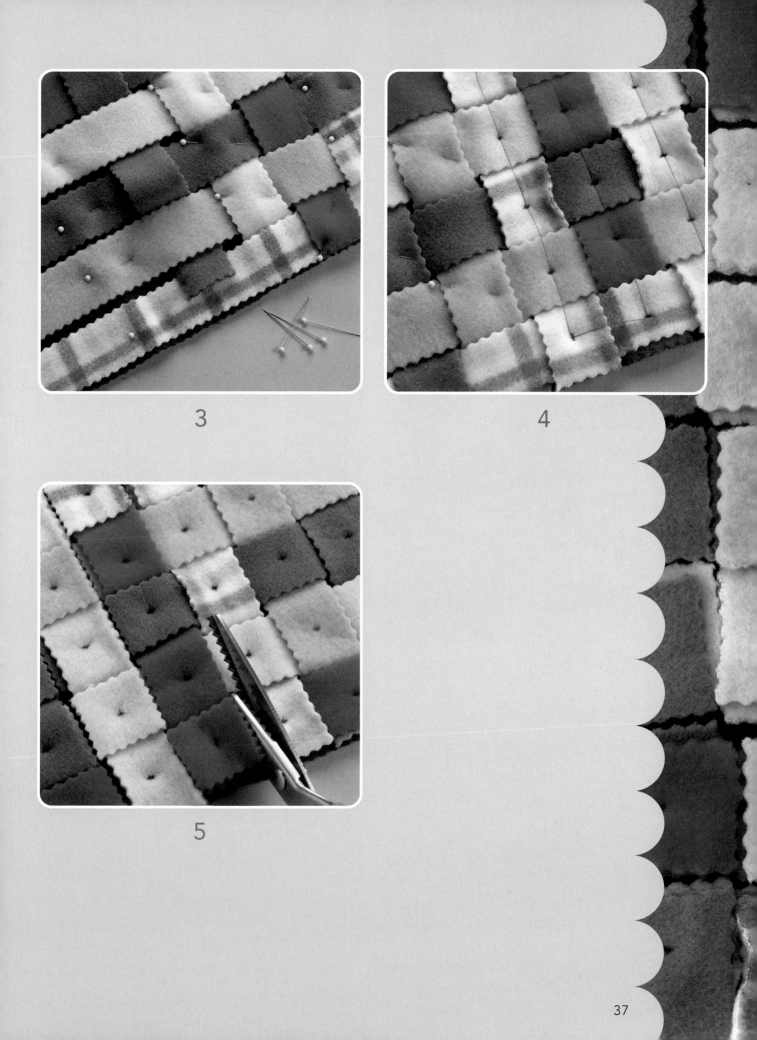

3

4

5

So many of us have discovered or rediscovered knitting that we included a project about knitting with fleece. You can create a ball of "yarn" that is super strong

Knit-with-Fleece Scarf

and easy to knit, using a rotary cutter and quilter's ruler. The fleece is cut in a continuous strip, then stretched and wound into a ball. The knitting pattern uses simple garter stitch and makes a scarf 30" (76 cm) long and 5½" (14 cm) wide with a keyhole opening on one end to slip the other end through.

MATERIALS

- ½ yd. (0.5 m) fleece
- Rotary cutter and cutting mat
- Masking tape, ½" (1.3 cm) wide
- Quilter's ruler
- Size 15 (10 mm) knitting needles
- Stitch holder

1. Lay out the fleece on a cutting mat. Trim any uneven edges so that you have a true rectangle. Fold the fleece carefully in half, right sides together, smoothing any wrinkles and matching selvages. Apply a strip of masking tape along the edge just inside the selvage. Fold in half again, bringing the first fold close to the inner edge of the masking tape.

2. Align ¼" (6 mm) mark on the quilter's ruler to the cut edge of the fleece. Using a rotary cutter, cut from the outer fold to the inner edge of the masking tape. Continue making ¼" (6 mm) cuts until all fabric has been cut into strips, connected at the selvage edges.

3. Cut away selvages close to the outer edge of the masking tape. Unfold the fabric and lay it flat. Carefully remove the masking tape. Clip through the uncut edge at one corner. Stretch the strip and begin winding it into a ball. Clip the opposite edge at the end of the second uncut slit. By cutting every other slit on alternating sides, you will create one continuous strip of "yarn." Continue to stretch and wind the yarn into a ball as you go along.

4. To knit the scarf, using size 15 (10 mm) needles, cast on 16 stitches. Work in garter stitch (knit every row) until the scarf is 4" (10 cm) from the beginning.

5. To create the slit, work only the first 8 stitches for 7 rows, and place the stitches on a holder. Join the yarn to the remaining 8 stitches and work the pattern for 7 rows.

6. Then continue to work across all 16 stitches until the scarf is 30" (76 cm) long. Bind off all stitches. Weave in the ends.

7. Trim away the little "nubbies" created by the double ends of the strips, if desired. Or leave them there for added texture.

2

3

5

This soft and stylish hat is reversible—it's two hats in one. It's crushproof, so you can stuff it

Reversible Cloche

into a pocket or bag and pull it out when it gets chilly. One size fits most adults and teens. Make it child-size simply by stitching deeper seams.

- Copy machine or graph paper for enlarging pattern
- ⅓ yd. (0.32 m) each of two coordinating, medium-weight fleeces
- Fabric marking pen or pencil
- Matching thread
- Yardstick (meterstick) or tape measure
- Hand-sewing needle

1. Enlarge the cloche pattern on page 100, and cut it out. Trace the pattern six times onto the fleece, with the direction of greatest stretch going crosswise, as indicated by the arrow on the pattern. Repeat with the coordinating fabric. Cut out the pieces along the traced lines.

2. Pin two pieces of the outer hat, wrong sides together, along one long curved edge. Stitch, beginning at the wide end. For an adult-size hat, use ¼" (6 mm) seam allowances throughout. To make a child-sized hat, sew ½" (1.3 cm) seams; then trim the seam allowances to ¼" (6 mm). Continue to join all six pieces. Repeat with the coordinating fabric pieces.

3. Pin one layer inside the other, wrong sides together, matching the seams. Stitch around the brim, ¼" (6 mm) from the edge, making sure that all the seam allowances are turned open. Sew six more concentric rings of stitching ¼" (6 mm) apart to form the hat brim, being careful to keep the seam allowances on both sides open and flat.

4. To make the reversible band and bow loop, layer the remaining fabrics wrong sides together. Cut a layered strip 1½" (3.8 cm) × the head circumference plus 3" (7.5 cm), with the greatest stretch going lengthwise. Also cut a layered 3" × 5" (7.5 × 12.7 cm) rectangle for the bow, with the greatest stretch in the longer direction. Round off the corners.

5. Sew the band strips together with ¼" (6 mm) seams on the long edges. Cut off a 3" (7.5 cm) segment from one end of the strip for the bow loop. Hand-stitch the cut ends together to form a loop. Slip the loop over the band and sew the ends of the band together.

6. Slide the loop to cover the seam in the band. Stitch the bow layers together ¼" (6 mm) from the edge. Fold a pleat into the center and insert the bow into the loop.

7. Slip the band onto the crown of the hat close to the point where the brim begins to flair. To reverse the hat or any of the parts, simply flip them over.

2

3

5

Total comfort meets total cute in these cropped and ruffled lounge pants perfect for a girly

Lazy Lounging Pants

girl slumber party or just relaxing in style. Basic cuffed PJ bottoms are transformed with some easy changes. A no-need-to-hem fleece ruffle adds panache, while contrasting grosgrain bows add the finishing touch.

MATERIALS

- McCall's® Endless Options pattern #3017, or similar pajama pants pattern
- Printed fleece (see pattern envelope for amount)
- Fabric marking pen or pencil
- ¼ yd. (0.25 m) contrast fleece for leg ruffles
- Yardstick (meterstick) or tape measure
- June Tailor® Fancy Fleece™ cutting ruler
- Matching thread
- 1 yd. (0.92 m) elastic, ⅜" (1 cm) wide
- Bodkin or safety pin
- 1 yd. (0.92 m) waistband elastic, ¾" (2 cm) wide
- 1¼ yd. (1.15 m) grosgrain ribbon, ⅝" (1.5 cm) wide
- 1¼ yd. (1.15 m) grosgrain ribbon, ¼" (6 mm) wide
- Rotary cutter and cutting mat

1. Pin the pants front pattern over the pants back pattern, aligning the side seam lines of the appropriate size. Match the lines at the hip and down the leg, and disregard slight curve at the waist. Alter the pattern as necessary for length and waistline placement. Mark the waistline cutting line 1⅜" (3.5 cm) above the natural waistline. Pin the pattern to a double layer of fleece, and cut out the fleece, cutting one piece for each front and back leg. Mark the front and back to avoid confusion later.

2. Measure the lower edge of one pants leg piece. Cut two strips of the contrast fleece this length and 4½" (11.5 cm) wide. Cut one edge of each strip in scallops, using the Fancy Fleece cutting ruler.

3. Pin a scalloped strip to the lower edge of each leg piece, right sides together and matching straight edges. Stitch together in a ⅝" (1.5 cm) seam.

4. Trim away the pants fabric seam allowance close to the stitching. Turn the scalloped strip down, turning the remaining seam allowance to the underside. Stitch close to the edge of the seam allowance, creating a casing for elastic.

5. Measure around the leg at the point where the elastic will be. Cut two pieces of ⅜" (1 cm) elastic 1½" (3.8 cm) longer than this measurement. Thread elastic through the casings, using a bodkin or safety pin, and pin at the ends to secure.

6. Sew the inner leg seams, catching the elastic ends in the stitching. Stitch again over the casing ends to secure the elastic.

7. Place one leg inside the other, right sides together, and stitch the crotch seam, leaving a 1" (2.5 cm) opening at the front, 1½" (3.8 cm) from the top.

8. Turn under the upper edge 1⅜" (3.5 cm) and stitch close to the lower edge. Stitch again ¼" (6 mm) from the upper fold, forming a casing with the opening at the front right side.

9. Cut a piece of ¾" (2 cm) elastic 6" (15 cm) shorter than the waistline. Cut the wider grosgrain ribbon in half and stitch one piece securely to each end of the elastic. Thread the ribbon and elastic into the casing, using a bodkin or safety pin. Tie the ribbon into a bow.

10. Cut the narrower grosgrain ribbon in half. Tie each piece into a bow, and tack the bows to the outside of the pants legs at the casings.

2

4

6

9

This uptown set is the ultimate
fantasy dress-up look for a diva
in training. It features hot pink

Glam Muff and Capelet

furry fleece. Muff and capelet
can be made in just a few hours.

Muff

1. Cut a piece of furry fleece 18" long × 11¼" wide (46 × 28.7 cm) for the outer muff. Cut a piece of coordinating fleece for the lining 13¼" long × 9¼" wide (33.7 × 23.6 cm). Cut a piece of upholstery batting 13¼" × 8" (33.7 × 20.5 cm).

2. Sew gathering stitches within the ½" (1.3 cm) seam allowances on both long sides of the outer muff. Pin the short ends right sides together, and stitch. Stitch the short ends of the lining piece right sides together. Stitch around the circular end of the lining on the seam line.

3. Turn the lining right side out and slip it into the outer muff. Pin the circular ends of the muff and lining pieces, right sides together, matching the seams. Pull up the gathering threads on the muff to ease in the fullness. Stitch.

4. Fold the ribbon in half, forming a loop, and pin the ends to the right side of the muff at the seam on the unstitched end. Stitch across the ribbon ends securely.

5. Roll the batting into a tube and hand-stitch the edges together.

6. With the muff and lining both inside out, slide your arm through the muff and lining. Slide the batting tube over the lining. Pull the outer muff over the batting.

7. Pull up the gathering threads on the outer muff to ease in the fullness. Turn under the lining edge on the stitching line, and pin it over the gathers, matching seams and pulling lining firmly into place. The ribbon loop should be on the outside. Hand-stitch the lining in place.

Capelet

1. Cut a piece of furry fleece for the outer capelet 33" wide × 9" long (84 × 23 cm). Cut a matching piece of coordinating fleece for the lining. Also cut two pieces of coordinating fleece 30" wide × 8" long (76 × 20.5 cm) for the ties.

2. On the wrong side of the outer capelet piece, mark points 5" (12.7 cm) from each corner on the long edges and 2" (5 cm) from each corner on the short edges. Draw curved lines to connect the marks at each corner. Trim the lining piece to match.

3. Fold a tie in half lengthwise, right sides together. Cut one end diagonally. Sew a ½" (1.3 cm) seam on the long edges and the angled end. Repeat for the other tie. Trim the seam allowances and turn the ties right side out.

4. Pin the ties to the center of the capelet ends, right sides together. Baste in place. Roll the ties up and pin them in place to prevent them from getting caught when you sew the lining seam.

5. Pin the lining to the outer capelet, right sides together and edges even. Sew a ½" (1.3 cm) seam all around, leaving a 6" (15 cm) opening in the lower edge for turning. Turn the capelet right side out and slipstitch the opening closed.

3

5

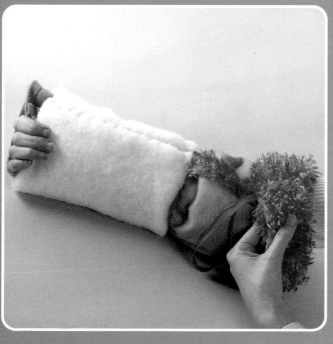

6

This ultimate security blanket comforts baby with the softness of thick fleece and the cool smoothness of satin. It is sized

Tagalong Blankie

small to go everywhere, which is where babies and toddlers want to take their blankies. The cushy fleece is double-sided and two-toned. You can whip up a blankie in just a few hours. Personalize it with the appliquéd name tag if you like.

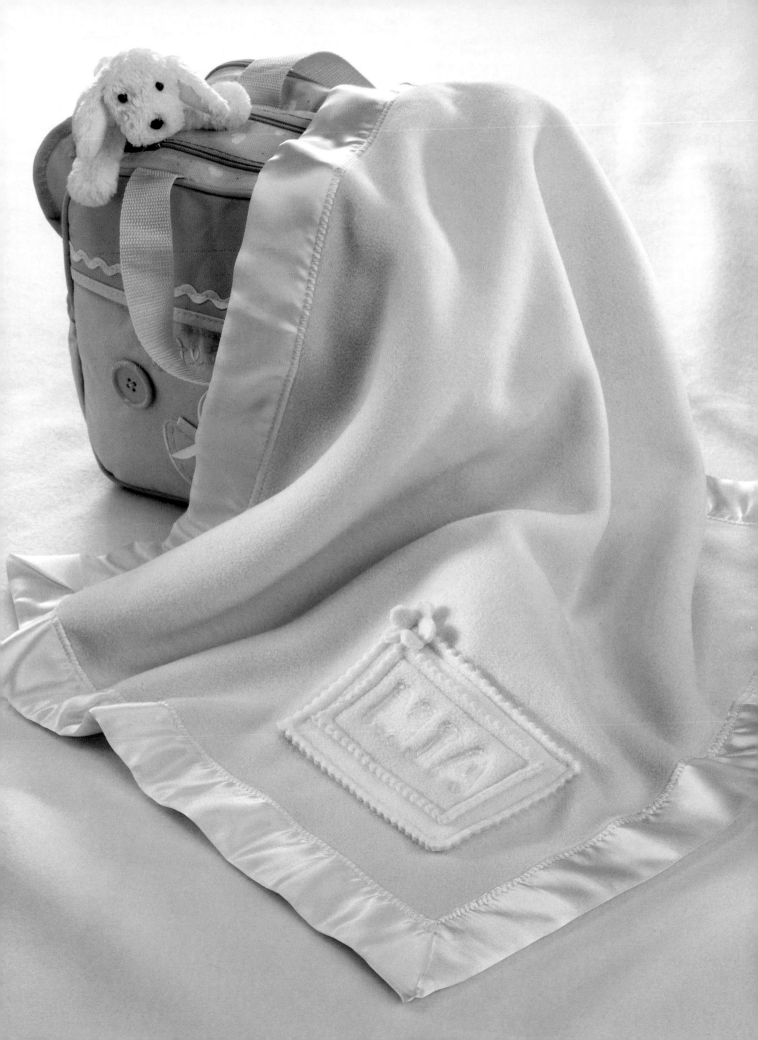

MATERIALS

- ¾ yd. (0.7 m) two-toned, double-sided fleece
- Quilter's ruler or T-square
- One package coordinating blanket binding
- Matching thread
- Iron
- Fabric glue stick
- Paper for tracing pattern
- Fabric marking pen or pencil
- Pinking shears or pinking rotary cutter and cutting mat
- Temporary spray adhesive, such as Sulky KK2000

1. Cut out a perfect 24" (61 cm) square of the fleece, using a quilter's ruler or T-square for accuracy. Avoid cutting too close to the selvage where the fabric might ripple.

2. Slip the blanket edge between the layers of the binding, beginning near the center of one side and going clockwise to the first corner. Tuck the edge in as close as possible to the binding fold, and pin in place. Stitch along the edge of the binding using the widest zigzag stitch; the left-hand stitches should go just off the edge of the binding. Stop at the corner, securing with a backstitch.

3. Remove the blanket from the sewing machine. Open out the binding at the corner and fold it diagonally so the next edge of the blanket aligns to the binding fold. Press the diagonal fold lightly with tip of iron.

4. Fold the binding closed so that the angled fold forms a mitered corner. The fold runs diagonally from the outer corner to the inner corner, matching up perfectly. Flip the blanket over and match up the mitered corner edges on the back as well, securing with the glue stick.

5. Pin the binding in place to the next corner. Place the blanket under the presser foot at the inner corner of the miter. Backstitch to secure and continue stitching with a wide zigzag stitch to the next corner.

6. Repeat steps 2 to 5 on the remaining sides and corners. When you reach the side where you started, cut the binding 4" (10 cm) beyond the beginning. Open out the fold, and press under 2" (5 cm) at the end. Reposition the binding and finish stitching it in place, stopping 1" (2.5 cm) past the overlap; backstitch. Then tack in place over the folded end to secure.

7. To personalize the quilt with reverse appliqué, enlarge the desired letters from the patterns (page 103) and trace them onto plain paper, leaving about ¼" (6 mm) between letters. Draw a rectangle about ½" (1.3 cm) beyond the edges of the letters, and cut out the rectangle. Use it to mark a rectangle on a piece of fleece; cut out the fleece with pinking shears or a pinking rotary cutter. Cut a second rectangle of fleece 1" (2.5 cm) larger than first rectangle.

8. Center the smaller piece over the larger piece, reversing the colors; pin. Stitch around the rectangle ¼" (6 mm) from the pinked edge of the inner rectangle.

9. Adhere the paper pattern onto the inner rectangle, using temporary spray adhesive. Stitch each letter, following the lines on the paper. Tear away the paper pattern.

10. Using sharp pointed scissors, cut away the top layer of fabric inside each letter close to the stitching to reveal the contrasting layer beneath.

11. Pin the appliqué to the lower right corner of the blanket. Stitch around the outer edge of the appliqué ¼" (6 mm) from the pinked edge. To add a dimensional embellishment, cut out a simple fleece flower. Stitch the flower center to the upper left corner of the appliqué. If the blanket is for a baby boy, you might prefer to use a star shape instead.

3

4

9

10

This quartet of baby bunnies will bring giggles of delight to that little bundle of joy in your life. The soft squishy ears are just the right size for a tiny grasp. You

Baby Bunnies

can make these sweet toys quickly and easily from leftover fleece scraps or coordinate fabrics with a favorite blanket. Each bunny has a hand-stitched face and a jaunty little hat that can be styled to create various bunny characters from cowboys to southern belles. Use soft medium to lightweight fleece.

MATERIALS

- Paper for tracing pattern
- Two matching pieces of fleece about 8" × 10" (20.5 × 25.5 cm) plus two contrasting 5" (12.7 cm) pieces for the hat, for each bunny
- Fabric marking pen or pencil
- 2½" (6.5 cm) square of fusible tricot interfacing
- Iron
- Embroidery floss and hand embroidery needle
- Matching thread
- 1 oz. (30 g) polyester fiberfill
- Compass
- Pinking shears or pinking rotary cutter and cutting mat

1. Trace the pattern on page 104, and cut it out. Pin two pieces of fleece, right sides together. Trace the bunny pattern on the fleece and cut them out.

2. Fuse a 2½" (6.5 cm) square of tricot interfacing onto the wrong side of the bunny front behind the face. Use a warm iron and light touch.

3. Transfer the embroidery pattern and hand-embroider the bunny's face.

4. Fold the lower corners of the bunny front, aligning the edges. Stitch ¼" (6 mm) seams. Repeat for the bunny back.

5. Pin the front to the back, right sides together, aligning the lower corner seams. Stitch ¼" (6 mm) seam all around, leaving an opening at the bottom for turning. Clip between the ears close to the stitching line.

6. Turn the bunny right side out. Pinch each ear to form a pleat. Hand-tack near the bottom of the ears, pulling the ears together.

7. Stuff the bunny with polyester fiberfill. Hand-stitch the opening closed.

8. Draw a circle with a 4½" (11.5 cm) diameter for the hat pattern and cut it out. Use the pattern to trace two contrasting hat pieces. Cut them out, using pinking shears or a pinking rotary cutter.

9. Mark a 1" (2.5 cm) circle in the center of each hat. Mark a dot on the center circle and draw lines at right angles to each other from the dot to the outer edge of the hat for a dart. Place the hats right sides together and stitch the center circle. Cut out the circle close to the stitching line.

10. Stitch the darts, and trim the fabric close to the stitching.

11. Turn the hat right side out, aligning the darts. Stitch the layers together ¼" (6 mm) from the pinked edge.

12. Pull the bunny ears through the hole in the center of the hat and turn back the hat brim as desired.

2

6

10

This textural play mat, a baby-sized take on the traditional bearskin rug, will provide hours of fun for baby and oodles of

Bearskin Play Rug

great photo ops for adoring parents, grandparents, and aunties. The cuddly bear features thick, silky, furry-fleece fabric with a generous layer of soft batting inside. Simply turn it over for a mat that's all fur; the bear's head flips around so the face is always smiling at you.

MATERIALS

- Copy machine or graph paper for enlarging pattern
- Paper for tracing pattern
- Fabric marking pen or pencil
- 1 yd. (0.92 m) solid-color plain fleece
- 1 yd. (0.92 m) matching furry fleece
- Temporary spray adhesive
- 1 yd. (0.92 m) high-loft batting
- Ruler
- 6" × 8" (15 × 20.5 cm) scrap of black fleece or felt for eyes, nose, and mouth
- Thread, matching and black
- Hand-sewing needle

1. Enlarge the body, head, and tail patterns on pages 105 and 106, and cut them out. Transfer all markings onto the pattern paper. Cut out the paws, tummy, ears, and muzzle, saving the pieces to use for patterns. Also trace and cut out the tail pattern on page 106.

2. Trace the front body onto the right side of the plain fleece and cut it out. Also trace the cutout areas.

3. Trace two tails, four paws, a tummy, two ears, and a muzzle on the wrong side of the furry fleece. Cut them out. Use temporary spray adhesive to secure the tummy and paws to the right side of the body front. Sew around each shape with a wide zigzag stitch.

4. Pin two tails right sides together; place them over two 5" (12.7 cm) squares of batting. Sew a ½" (1.3 cm) seam around the curved edge, leaving the straight edge open. Trim the batting close to the stitching; trim the seam allowances to ¼" (6 mm). Turn the tail right side out. Stitch across the open end with zigzag stitches. Pin the tail in place on the bear front, matching raw edges; stitch.

5. Place the bear front over the furry fleece, right sides together, with the tail tucked in. Layer the bear pieces over batting. Pin carefully all around. Sew a ½" (1.3 cm) seam around the bear, leaving the neck open. Trim the seam allowances to ¼" (6 mm). Turn the bear right side out.

6. Trace the head pattern onto the right side of the plain fleece. Trace the cutout areas. Cut out the head.

7. Use temporary spray adhesive to secure the ears and muzzle to the face. Sew around each shape with a wide zigzag stitch.

8. Trace and cut out the patterns for the eyes and nose; cut them from the black fleece or felt. Also cut a ¼" × 3" (6 mm × 7.5 cm) strip for the line from the nose to the mouth and a ¼" × 5" (6 mm × 12.7 cm) strip for the mouth. Pin the features in place on the face.

9. Change the sewing machine thread to black and stitch around the eyes and nose with medium zigzag stitch. Set the machine to the widest zigzag stitch, and sew the fleece line from the nose to the mouth; then sew over the mouth, backstitching to secure.

10. Place the head front over the furry fleece, right sides together. Layer the head pieces over two layers of batting. Pin all around. Stitch ½" (1.3 cm) from the cut edge. Do not leave an opening for turning. Trim the batting close to the stitching. Trim the seam allowances to ¼" (6 mm) and clip close to the stitching at the ears.

11. Cut a 5" (12.7 cm) horizontal slit through the batting and furry fleece in the center back of the head. Turn the head right side out through the slit. Topstitch across the bottom of the ears.

12. Insert the neck into the slit on the back of the head, fur sides together. Stitch in place by machine, using a narrow seam allowance. Turn the head down and hand-stitch the other side in place.

3

4

9

1

Your preschooler will love this playful nap quilt. Made from colorful and fluffy double-sided fleece, it's even more cushy

Dinosaur Nap Quilt

because there is a generous double layer of thick batting inside. The friendly stegosaurus's spines are fun to make using a special no-sew cut and turn technique. When not in use, the mat can be rolled up and tucked inside the dinosaur.

Purple

balloon   sweater

monkey   grapes

ears

MATERIALS

- Copy machine or graph paper for enlarging pattern
- 2½ yd. (2.3 m) double-sided fleece
- Fabric marking pen or pencil
- 1 package high-loft batting
- Matching thread
- Pinking shears or pinking rotary cutter and cutting mat
- 26" (66 cm) Velcro®, 1" (2.5 cm) wide

1. Enlarge the patterns on pages 107, 108, and 109, and transfer all markings onto the pattern paper.

2. Trace the foot pattern four times on one side of a piece of fleece. Layer this piece over another piece, same color facing up, with a layer of batting between them; pin. Stitch on the marked lines. Cut the feet apart, leaving wide margins all around. Trim away the batting close to the stitching, but don't trim the fabric.

3. Stitch again ¼" (6 mm) outside the first stitching lines, encasing the batting edge. Use the presser foot as a guide to maintain an equal margin all around. Cut out the feet close to the outer stitching line, using pinking shears or a pinking rotary cutter.

4. Prepare the tail spines, following the method in steps 2 and 3, but omitting batting. Stitch a line down the center of each. Prepare the tail, following steps 2 and 3, with the same color facing out on both sides but in the first stitching line, leave an opening for the tail spines. Fold each spine in half at an angle, and pin them into the opening. Sew the opening closed and finish the tail.

5. Sew the head, following the method in steps 2 and 3, with the same color facing out on both sides. Cut two scraps of fleece for the eyes; mark the eye circle on the reverse side of one piece. Pin the eye scraps, reverse side out, over the eye location on the head. Stitch around the eye through all layers, and trim close to the stitching on both sides. Sew the mouth using a short, narrow zigzag stitch.

6. Cut out two body pieces and two body lining pieces from the fleece. Cut two body linings from the batting. Mark the stitching lines and spine cutting lines on the right side of one body piece.

7. Place a lining, reverse side up, over the reverse side of a body piece, with a batting piece between them. The lower hem edge of the body piece should extend 1¾" (4.5 cm) below the lining and batting. Turn up the hem of the body over the lower edge of the lining. Stitch the hem in place, beginning and ending ½" (1.3 cm) from the sides. Repeat for the remaining body, batting, and lining.

8. Center the loop side of the Velcro over the inside of one hem, and stitch in place along both edges.

Continued on page 70

2

3

4

8

9. Layer the body pieces, lining sides together. Insert the head and tail where marked. Pin. Stitch on the marked stitching line.

10. Trim away the batting and lining of the body close to the stitching, but don't trim the outer fabric, head, or tail. Stitch again ¼" (6 mm) outside the first stitching lines, encasing the trimmed edges.

11. Cut the front and back on the spine cutting lines. Cut the ends of each spine into a point. Cut a small hole in the center of each spine near the seam line. Working with one layer, bring the spine point forward and through the hole. Pull it completely through and shape it. Repeat for each spine on one side. Then flip the dinosaur over and repeat with the other spines.

12. Cut two pieces each of fleece and batting 28" × 36" (71 × 91.5 cm) for the nap pad. Pin the fleece, reverse sides together, with two layers of batting underneath. Sew a ½" (1.3 cm) seam around three sides, leaving one narrow end open. Trim the seam allowances close to the stitching. Turn the nap pad right side out. Topstitch the open edge closed, 1" (2.5 cm) from the edge. Trim away the batting from between the layers. Topstitch again ½" (1.3 cm) from the edge. Trim to ¼" (6 mm) using pinking shears or a pinking rotary cutter.

13. Center the hook side of the Velcro ¼" (6 mm) from the pinked edge, and stitch in place along both edges. To attach mat to the dinosaur, align the Velcro strips and press them together.

9

1

13

This tote features a dimensional appliqué created by layering colors and textures to form an all-over bamboo pattern. Lined with a coordinating cotton print,

Elegant Bamboo Tote

it features a generous inside pocket to hold keys, phone, and other small essentials. The tote is perfect for carrying knitting or stitching projects around, too. Purchased bamboo handles complete the look. The appliqué would also be perfect on a pillow cover, giving contemporary décor an Asian accent.

MATERIALS

- Yardstick (meterstick) or tape measure
- 1½ yd. (1.4 m) persimmon heather ribbed fleece
- ½ yd. (0.5 m) basil green fleece
- Paper for tracing pattern
- 1 yd. (0.92 m) very stiff interfacing, such as Timtex, 18" (46 cm) wide
- 1 yd. (0.92 m) printed cotton fabric, 45" (115 cm) wide, for lining
- Paper for tear-away stabilizer
- Temporary spray adhesive
- Matching thread
- Open-toe embroidery foot, optional
- Chenille rotary cutting tool, optional
- Pair bamboo tote handles

1. From the ribbed fleece, cut two pieces 13½" wide × 16½" long (34.3 × 41.8 cm) for the tote front and back. Cut four pieces 4" wide × 9" long (10 × 23 cm) for the handle straps. Cut a strip 4" wide × 45½" long (10 × 116 cm) for the sides and bottom gusset.

2. From the green fleece, cut one piece 13½" × 16½" (34.3 × 41.8 cm) for the bamboo appliqué. Enlarge the leaf pattern on page 110, and cut it out; cut out 10 green fleece leaves.

3. From the interfacing, cut two pieces 12½" × 15½" (31.8 × 39.3 cm) for the front and back. Cut one piece 12½" × 3½" (31.8 × 9 cm) for the bottom, and two pieces 15½" × 3½" (39.3 × 9 cm) for the sides.

4. From the lining fabric, cut two pieces 13½" × 16½" (34.3 × 41.8 cm) for the front and back. Cut one piece 4" × 45½" (10 × 116 cm) for the gusset. Cut four pieces 4" × 9" (10 × 23 cm) for the handle straps. Cut one piece 8½" × 12" (21.8 × 30.5 cm) for the pocket.

5. Enlarge the bamboo appliqué pattern (page 110) and trace it onto paper for a tear-away stabilizer. Center the front interfacing piece on the wrong side of the tote front, and pin in place. Center the green appliqué piece, right side up, over the right side of the tote front, and pin in place. Attach the traced pattern over the green fleece, using temporary spray adhesive.

6. Thread the sewing machine with green thread and attach an open-toe embroidery foot, if you have one, to aid visibility. Straight stitch around each bamboo section, backstitching at the beginning and end of each shape.

7. Tear away the paper stabilizer. Trim away excess fabric close to the stitching lines, using sharp pointed scissors. A chenille rotary cutting tool is helpful for cutting between the bamboo sections.

8. Using the photo as a guide, fold each leaf into a V shape and pin it to the appliqué with the center of the V touching a joint between bamboo sections. Stitch each leaf set from one point to the center of the V. Leave the needle down in the fabric to pivot, fold away the excess fabric inside the angle, then stitch to the other point. Backstitch at the beginning and end.

9. To sculpt the leaves, pull the excess fabric inside the angle to the outer point of the V, making the leaf edges roll. Stitch in place. Repeat for all the leaf sets.

Continued on page 76

7

8

9

10. Spray one side of the remaining interfacing pieces with temporary adhesive, and center them on the wrong side of the tote back and gusset. There should be a ½" (1.3 cm) margin around the tote back. On the gusset, the fabric should extend ½" (1.3 cm) at the ends and there should be equal, narrow gaps between the bottom and side pieces.

11. Pin the gusset to the tote front, right sides together, matching edges and corners. Clip into the seam allowance of the gusset at the lower corners to allow the gusset to turn the corner smoothly. Stitch a ½" (1.3 cm) seam on the sides and bottom. Repeat to attach the tote back.

12. Pin a fleece handle strap and lining handle strap right sides together. Stitch ½" (1.3 cm) seams on the long edges. Turn the strap right side out. Press lightly with a warm iron on the lining side. Repeat for the remaining handle straps.

13. Fold the straps in half, lining sides together. Pin two straps to each side of the tote top, even with the side seams, matching upper edges. Stitch in place ½" (1.3 cm) from the edge.

14. Fold the lining pocket in half crosswise, right sides together. Stitch ½" (1.3 cm) seams on the sides and bottom, leaving an opening on the bottom for turning. Trim the corners diagonally. Turn the pocket right side out, and press.

15. Pin the pocket to the right side of one large lining piece, centered 3" (7.5 cm) below the upper edge. Stitch in place along the sides and bottom, backstitching at the beginning and end.

16. Stitch the lining pieces together as in step 11 . Turn under the upper edge ½" (1.3 cm) and press.

17. Turn the handle straps upward, also turning the upper edge of the tote under ½" (1.3 cm). Slip the lining into the tote. Pin the upper folded edges together. Stitch ¼" (6 mm) from the edges. Then stitch again ¼" (6 mm) from the first stitching.

18. Insert the bamboo handles into the straps. Pin the straps together close to the handles. Remove the handles. Stitch across the straps as pinned to make casings for the handles. Insert the handles again.

15

17

18

Here's a thoughtful gift for your favorite golfer. This trio of argyle print fleece golf club covers

Golf Club Covers Gift Set

features reverse appliqué numbers and a cushiony extra layer of fleece lining to protect those all-important woods.

MATERIALS

- Copy machine or graph paper for enlarging pattern
- ½ yd. (0.5 m) medium-weight fleece (argyle print)
- ½ yd. (0.5 m) coordinating solid-color fleece for lining
- Fabric marking pen or pencil
- Small amount of contrasting fleece for numbers
- Ruler
- Paper for tracing pattern
- Temporary spray adhesive, such as Sulky KK2000
- Open-toe embroidery foot, optional
- Matching thread
- Pinking shears or pinking rotary cutter and cutting mat
- ⅔ yd. (0.63 m) elastic, ⅜" (1 cm) wide
- Bodkin or safety pin

1. Enlarge the patterns on page 111, and cut them out. Cut a front and back for each club cover from the argyle fleece. Also cut a front and back for each club cover from the lining fleece. Mark the appliqué placement on the right side of the cover front. Mark stitching lines for the elastic casing on the lining pieces.

2. For each club cover, cut a 6" (15 cm) square of the contrasting solid-color fleece and the lining fleece. To make number appliqués, trace the numbers from the patterns onto paper. Use temporary spray adhesive to hold the paper in place in the center of a lining fleece square; layer the contrasting square underneath.

3. Attach an open-toe embroidery foot, if you have one, and straight stitch carefully around the outlines of the numbers. Pivot at the corners, leaving the needle down in the fabric.

4. Tear away the paper. Carefully cut away the inside of the number, cutting through the top layer only close to the stitching.

5. Draw a 3¼" (8.2 cm) circle around the number with a fabric marking pen or pencil, centering the number in the circle. Cut out the circle through both layers, and trim away ¼" (6 mm) from the underlayer.

6. Spray the back of the appliqué with temporary adhesive, and affix it to the cover front. Stitch around the outer edge of the appliqué with a medium width zigzag stitch.

7. Pin the cover front to the back, right sides together. Stitch a ¼" (6 mm) seam. Repeat for the lining, leaving the seam open at the casing markings on one side. Trim all layers close to the stitching. Turn the lining right side out.

8. Slip the cover inside the lining, wrong sides together, matching seams. Pin the lower edges together. Stitch ½" (1.3 cm) from the edge. Trim close to the stitching using pinking shears or a pinking rotary cutter to trim close to stitching.

9. Slide the club cover onto the free arm of the sewing machine, lining side out. Stitch on the marked casing lines all around the club cover. Remove the cover from the machine. Cut a 7" (18 cm) piece of elastic. Use a bodkin or safety pin to insert the elastic through the casing. Overlap the ends and stitch them together.

10. Ease the elastic back into the casing, distributing the gathers evenly. Turn the cover right side out. Turn up the contrasting cuff.

3

4

9

You'll warm a guy's heart as well as his hands when you give him these fleece shoveling mittens.

Toasty Shoveling Mittens

Features include stylish and practical palm patches of faux suede, toasty sherpa fleece lining, and snug ribbed cuffs to keep out the chill.

1. Enlarge the mitten patterns on page 112, and cut them out. Cut two mittens and two thumbs from the outer fleece; reserve a piece about 13" × 22" (33 × 56 cm) for the cuffs. Cut two mittens and two thumbs from the sherpa lining. Cut two palm patches of the suede. Be sure to turn the patterns over for lefts and rights. Transfer all pattern markings. Cut out thumb holes.

2. Fold an outer thumb in half, right sides together, and stitch a ¼" (6 mm) seam on the upper curve. Trim the seam allowances to ⅛" (3 mm).

3. Pin the thumb into the thumb hole of the mitten, right sides together, matching the thumb seam to the upper dot and aligning the lower dots. Stitch a ¼" (6 mm) seam. Trim the seam allowances to ⅛" (3 mm).

4. Repeat steps 2 and 3 for the other mitten and for the mitten linings. Stick the patches onto the right side of the mitten palms, using temporary spray adhesive, and stitch around each patch close to the edge.

5. Fold the mitten right sides together and stitch a ¼" (6 mm) seam on the side and upper curve. Trim the seam allowances to ⅛" (3 mm). Repeat for the other mitten and for the mitten linings. Turn the linings right side out.

6. Cut away the selvages from the reserved cuff fabric. To make continuous ribbing, thread your sewing machine with two spools of thread and insert a double needle. Place the fleece right side up under the presser foot so the first line of double-needle stitching will be one presser foot's width from the cut edge on the lengthwise grain. Stitch one row, stopping just before the end of the fabric. Loop the fabric around the free arm of the sewing machine from the back and align the cut edges, offsetting the alignment so the side of the front edge aligns to the first row of stitching.

7. Stitch continuously, keeping one presser foot's width of space between the rows, until all of the fabric has been sewn. Remove the fabric from the machine and cut the threads where the stitching crosses the butted edges to make a flat piece of ribbed fabric. Cut two cuffs 8" wide × 9" long (20.5 × 23 cm).

8. Fold a cuff in half vertically, right sides together, and stitch a ¼" (6 mm) seam. Trim the seam allowances to ⅛" (3 mm). Fold the cuff in half, wrong sides together, matching the seams. Place the cuff onto the free arm of the sewing machine and stitch the cut edges together, being careful not to stretch ribbing. Repeat for the other cuff.

9. Slip a lining over a mitten, wrong sides together. Slip a cuff inside the mitten, matching the side seams, and pin. Stitch all the layers together in a ½" (1.3 cm) seam. Trim the seam allowances of the lining and mitten close to the stitching.

10. Turn the cuff out, turning the cuff seam allowance over the trimmed seam allowances. Place the mitten wrong side out onto the free arm of the machine. Stitch again close to the edge of the cuff seam allowance, encasing the trimmed edges.

11. Repeat steps 9 and 10 for the other mitten. Turn the mittens right side out and start shoveling!

4

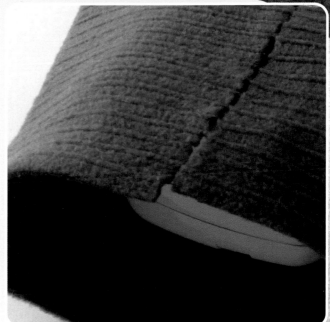

7

10

What a great way to create sunny warmth on a cold, dreary day! Our sunburst throw adds style, texture, and a splash of color to

Sunburst Throw

any casual décor. Dimensional cutwork squares of yellow fleece are embellished with glass beads and sewn directly onto a contrasting ultramarine blue background to form this eye-catching checkerboard throw.

MATERIALS

- ⅔ yd. (0.63 m) medium-weight yellow fleece
- Yardstick (meterstick) or tape measure
- Rotary cutter with scallop edge
- Cutting mat
- Fabric marking pen or pencil
- Quilter's ruler
- Rotary cutter with straight edge
- 72 blue glass beads, 6 mm
- Matching thread
- 1¼ yd. (1.15 m) medium-weight blue fleece
- Temporary spray adhesive, such as Sulky KK2000, optional
- Six yellow buttons, ⅞" (2.2 cm)
- June Tailor® Fringe Cut™ ruler

1. Cut six 12" (30.5 cm) squares of the yellow fleece, using the scallop-edge rotary cutter. Enlarge the pattern on page 108. Poke holes on the inner dots and dashes of the template. Place the template over one corner of a fleece square, and using a fabric marking pen or pencil, transfer the marks and the center point. Move the template and repeat in each quadrant of the square. Repeat for each square.

2. Align a quilter's ruler to the dots of one spoke in one fleece square. Using a rotary cutter with a straight edge, slit the fleece between the dots. Repeat for each spoke. Repeat for each square.

3. Pull together two adjacent cut edges, and hand-stitch a bead between the layers at the dashes. Knot securely and cut the thread close to the stitching. Repeat 11 times around the square. Repeat for each square.

4. Cut a 40" × 60" (102 × 152.5 cm) rectangle of the blue fleece, cutting away the selvages. Mark lines across the width of the fleece 4" (10 cm) from each end, at the center, and 12" (30.5 cm) above and below the center. Then mark lines lengthwise 2" (5 cm) from each side and 14" (35.5 cm) from each side.

5. Arrange the sunburst squares on the blue background in a checkerboard pattern using the marked lines as a guide. Use temporary spray adhesive or pins to secure. Stitch around each square ¼" (6 mm) from the edges.

6. From the remaining blue fleece, cut out six 2" (5 cm) circles using the scallop-edge rotary cutter. Use temporary spray adhesive or pins to secure a circle to the center of each sunburst square. Center a yellow button on top of each circle and hand-sew the button in place through all layers.

7. Place the end of the throw over a cutting board. Align the Fringe Cut ruler to the marked line at one end of the throw. Cut fringe, using the rotary cutter.

2

3

6

This oversized, overstuffed, and over-the-top designer pillow is sure to become a focal point of your décor. The cover comes off for easy care, making it the

Crazy Kaleidoscope Pillow

ultimate in art for every day. Start with a funky print fleece like this crazy quilt of designs and colors from the 70s. Manipulate the surface by adding dimensional appliqués, couching, and fleece chenille. Finish the pillow with a double row of highly textured, oversized cording and you've got wow!

MATERIALS

- 1½ yd. (1.4 m) paisley printed fleece

- ¾ yd. (0.7 m) each of two coordinating solid-color fleeces

- Yardstick (meterstick) or tape measure

- Fabric marking pen or pencil

- Matching thread

- Chenille rotary cutting tool

- 1 yd. (0.92 m) high-loft batting to make welting

- ½ yd. (0.5 m) ribbed fleece in coordinating color for outer welting

- 24" (61 cm) square pillow form

1. Cut two 16" (40.5 cm) squares of the print for the chenille squares and one 16" (40.5 cm) square from each of the two coordinating plain fleeces for backing the chenille squares.

2. Mark a diagonal line across the center of a print square. Layer the print square over a backing square, right sides facing up, and matching the directions of greatest stretch.

3. Stitch on the marked line. Then fill the square with parallel lines of stitching ½" (1.3 cm) apart, working from the center out on one side and then the other. Some distortion and shrinkage of the fabric will occur. This will be corrected in step 5.

4. Slit the top layer halfway between stitching rows, using a chenille rotary cutting tool.

5. Repeat steps 2 to 4 for the other chenille square. Trim the finished chenille squares to 14" (35.5 cm). Set aside.

6. Cut two 14" (35.5 cm) squares each of paisley print fleece for the appliqué squares, carefully selecting position of design elements in print for a pleasing composition. Also cut two 14" (35.5 cm) squares of a coordinating plain fleece for backing the appliqué squares. Layer the print squares over the backing squares, right sides facing up and matching the directions of greatest stretch.

7. Cut two 18" × 26" (46 × 66 cm) paisley pieces for the pillow back, and set them aside. From the remaining paisley fleece, cut out design elements and place them over matching elements on the fleece squares. Stitch the cutouts down, leaving the edges free to add dimension as in steps 8 to 10.

8. Cut ¼" (6 mm) strips of solid-color fleece on the crosswise grain. Pull a strip to stretch into "yarn." Using a zigzag stitch, couch the fleece yarn over a flower stem on the printed square.

9. Cut three or four of the narrow strips to 12" (30.5 cm), and pull the strips to curl them. Attach the curlicues to a printed square by stitching in the center of the cluster, leaving the curly ends free.

10. Cut a rectangle of striped fabric from the print. Stitch the piece onto a matching striped area, making pleats and tucks to create raised ridges.

11. Stitch an appliqué square to a chenille square, right sides together, using ½" (1.3 cm) seam allowance. Repeat with the remaining pair. Then sew the pairs together in a checkerboard patchwork.

Continued on page 94

4

8

9

10

12

15

12. Mark a point 6" (15 cm) from each corner on each side of the pillow front. Also mark points ½" (1.3 cm) from the corners. Trim away a sliver of fabric between the marks at each corner. This will prevent "ears" and help the pillow look more square when it is stuffed.

13. Cut a length of batting 6" (15 cm) × 99" (251.5 cm), piecing as necessary. Fold the strip in half lengthwise twice and pin the fold to the cut edges to form a batting core for fabric-covered welting. Stitch the fold to the cut edges with a zigzag stitch.

14. Cut 6" (15 cm) strips of ribbed fleece and piece them together with diagonal seams to a length of 99" (251.5 cm). Fold the strip around the batting core, aligning the cut edges. Stitch close to the core, using a zipper foot.

15. Cut 4" (10 cm) strips of solid-color fleece and piece them together with diagonal seams to a length of 99" (251.5 cm). Fold the strip in half lengthwise and pin it in place over the ribbed welting so the fold of the solid strip extends ½" (1.3 cm) over the previous stitching line. Stitch, using a zipper foot, over the previous stitching line. Trim away extra fabric of all layers, leaving ½" (1.3 cm) seam allowance.

16. Beginning in the center of one side, pin the double welting in place all around the pillow front, matching raw edges and clipping at corners as necessary. Sew the welting onto the pillow front, starting and stopping just short of the ends.

17. Cut the ends so they overlap 1½" (3.8 cm). Open the stitches. Trim away excess batting core so the ends just meet. Lap the ribbed fabric ends back over the batting core; lap the inner welt ends over each other. Finish stitching the welting in place.

18. On each pillow back piece, turn under one long edge 1" (2.5 cm) twice and stitch to make a hem.

19. Pin the pillow backs to the pillow front, right sides together, overlapping the backs to fit. Trim the corners of the backs to match the front. Sew the front and backs together, using a zipper foot to stitch close to the welting.

20. Turn the pillow cover right side out and insert the pillow form.

Patterns

Padded Hanger (enlarge 200%)

1 square = ½" (1.3 cm)

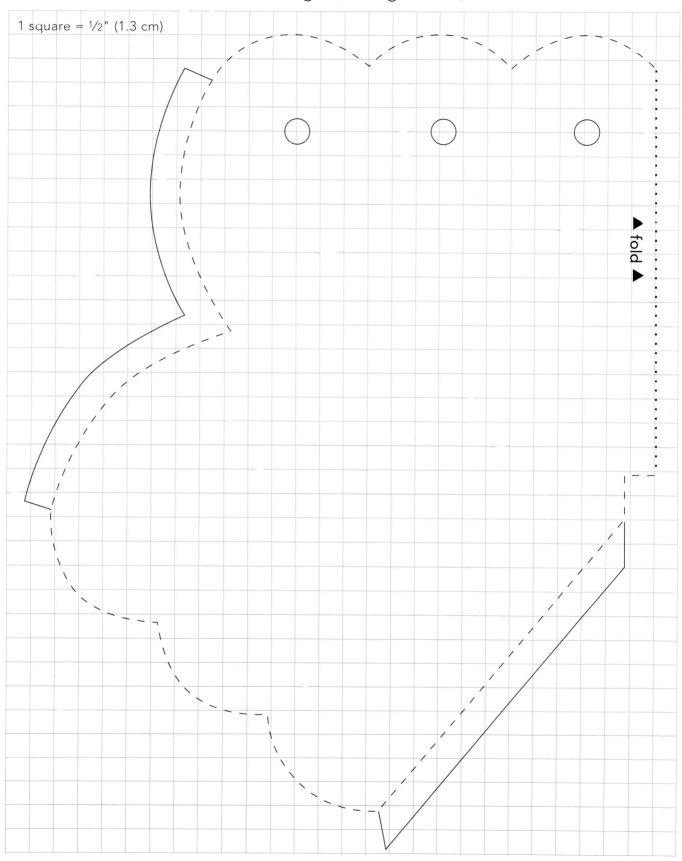

fold

Padded Hanger (full size)

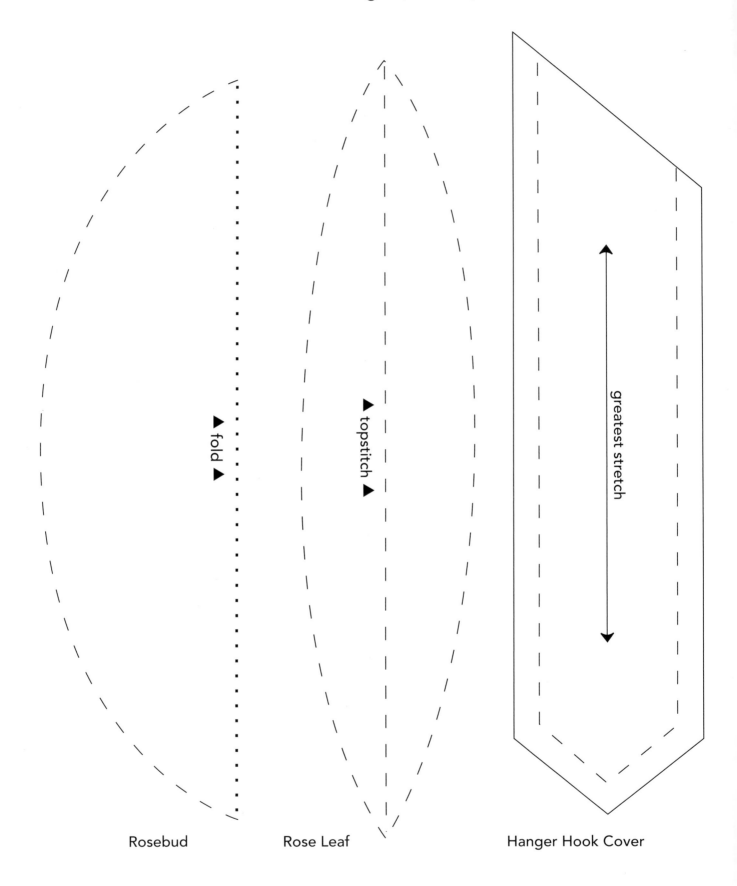

▶ fold ▶

▶ topstitch ▶

greatest stretch

Rosebud

Rose Leaf

Hanger Hook Cover

Lady Slipper Bow and Sole (enlarge 133%)

1 square = ½" (1.3 cm)

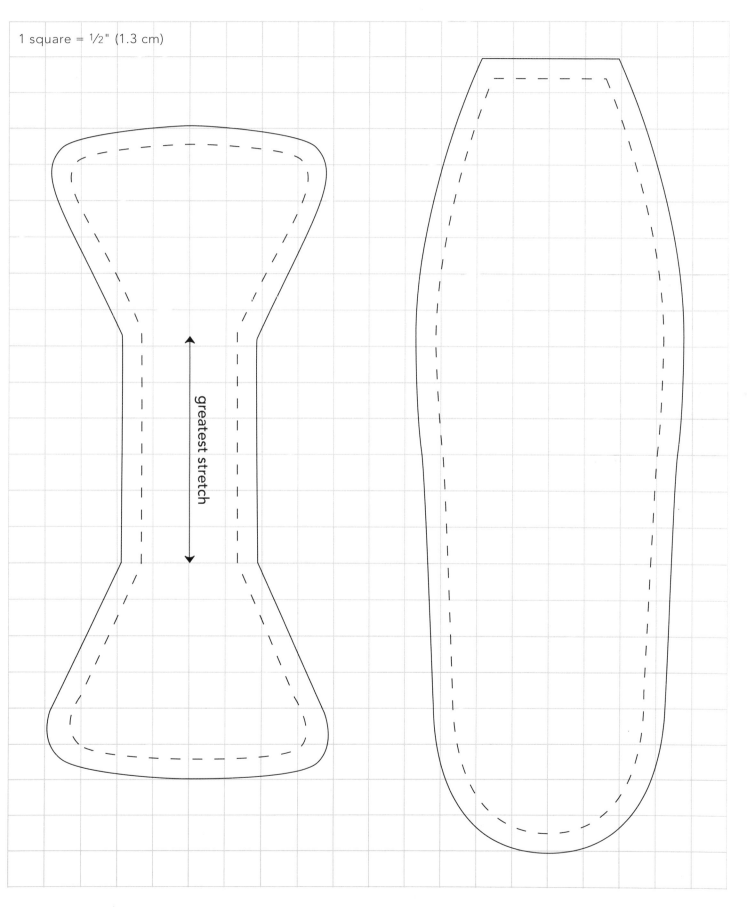

greatest stretch

Lady Slipper Upper (enlarge 133%)

1 square = ½" (1.3 cm)

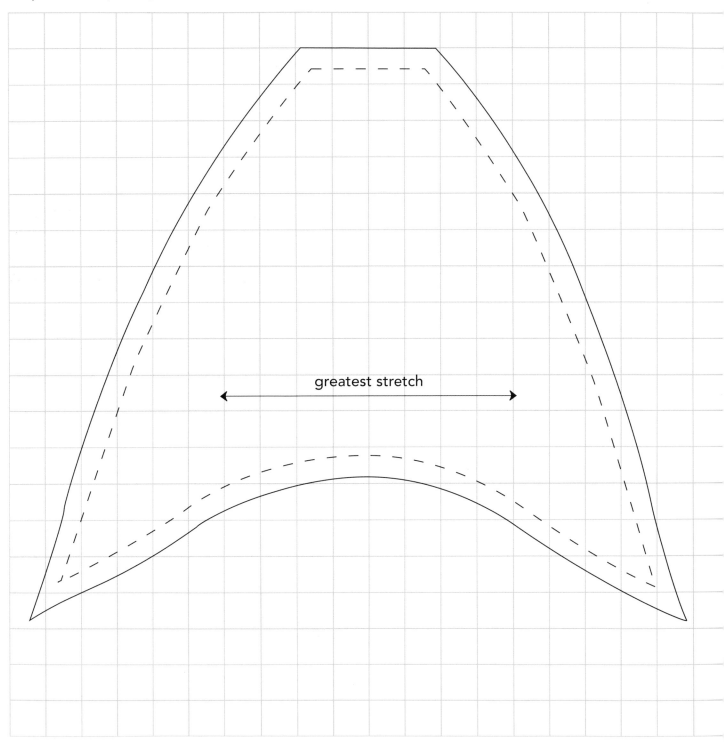

greatest stretch

Calla Lily (full size)

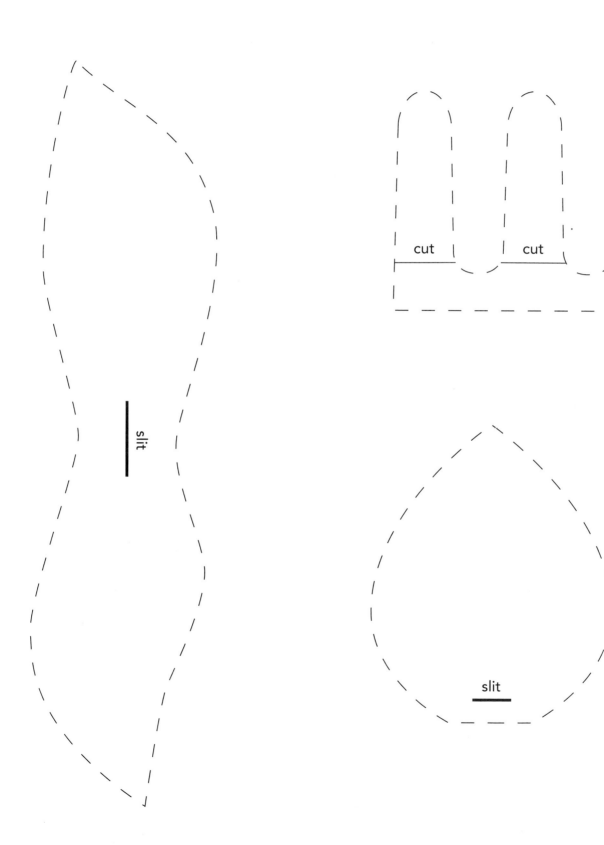

cut cut cut

slit

slit

Cloche (enlarge 133%)

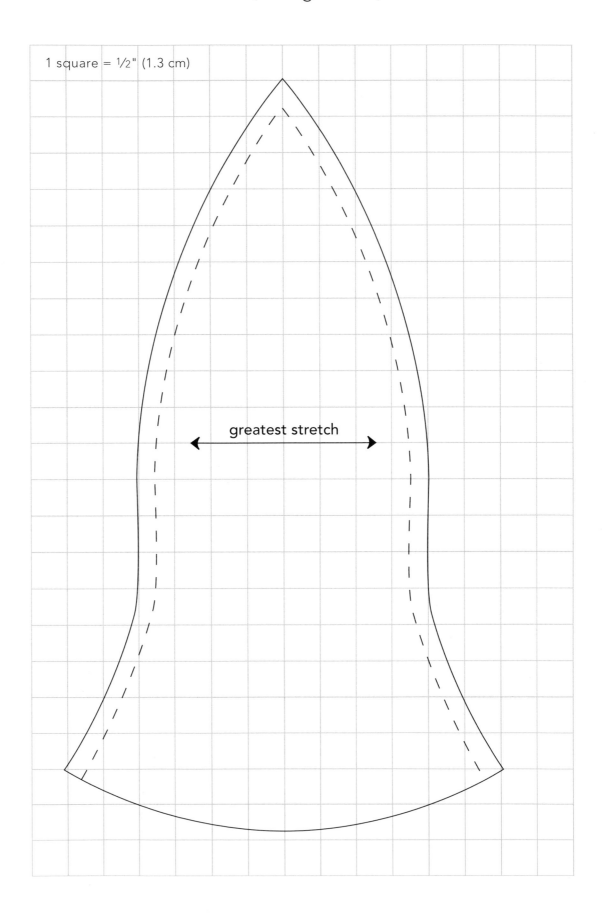

1 square = ½" (1.3 cm)

greatest stretch

Home Spa Booties (enlarge 200%)

1 square = ½" (1.3 cm)

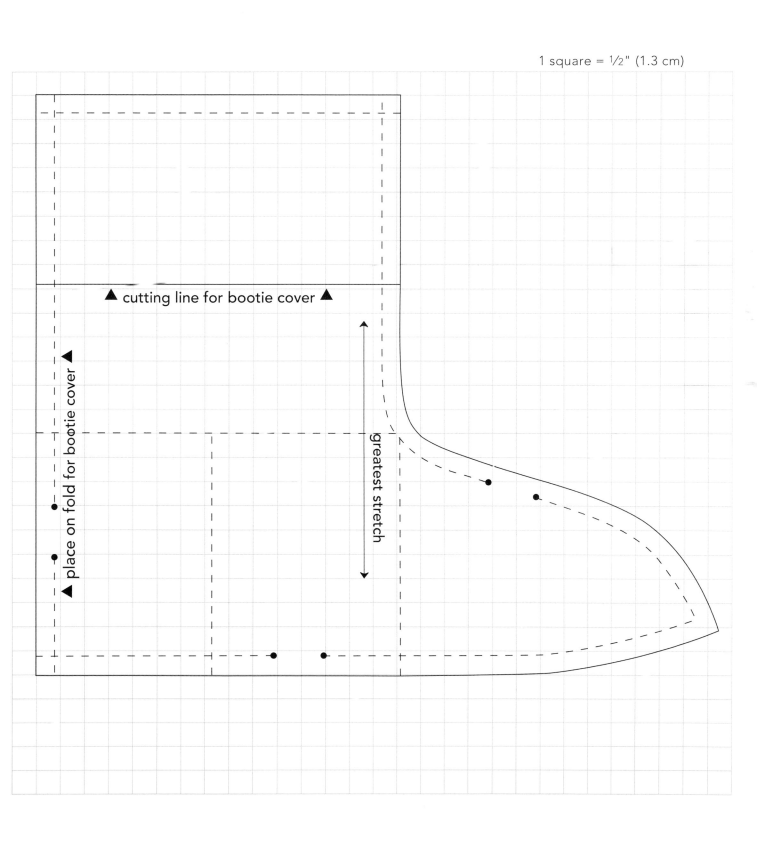

▲ cutting line for bootie cover ▲

◄ place on fold for bootie cover ◄

greatest stretch

Home Spa Booties Sole (enlarge 133%)

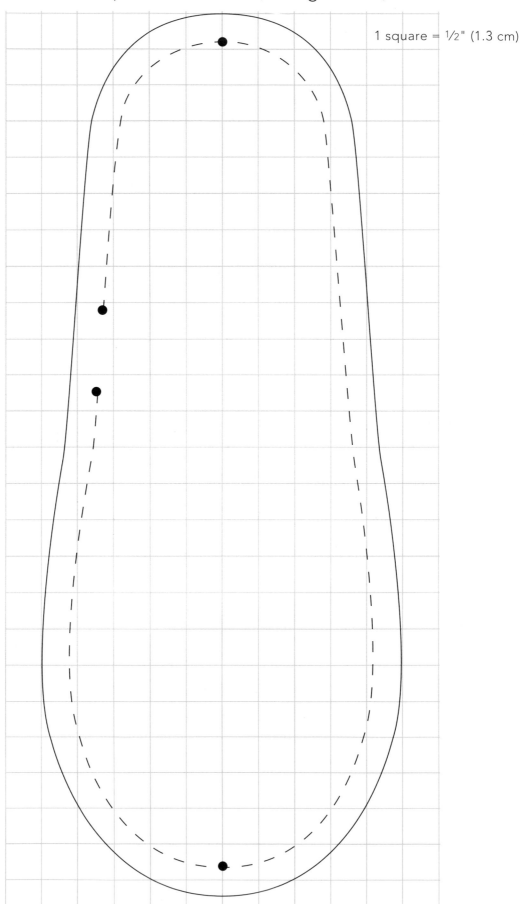

1 square = ½" (1.3 cm)

Tagalong Blankie Alphabet (enlarge 133%)

1 square = ½" (1.3 cm)

Baby Bunnies (full size)

Bearskin Rug Head (enlarge 133%)

1 square = ½" (1.3 cm)

▲ fold ▲

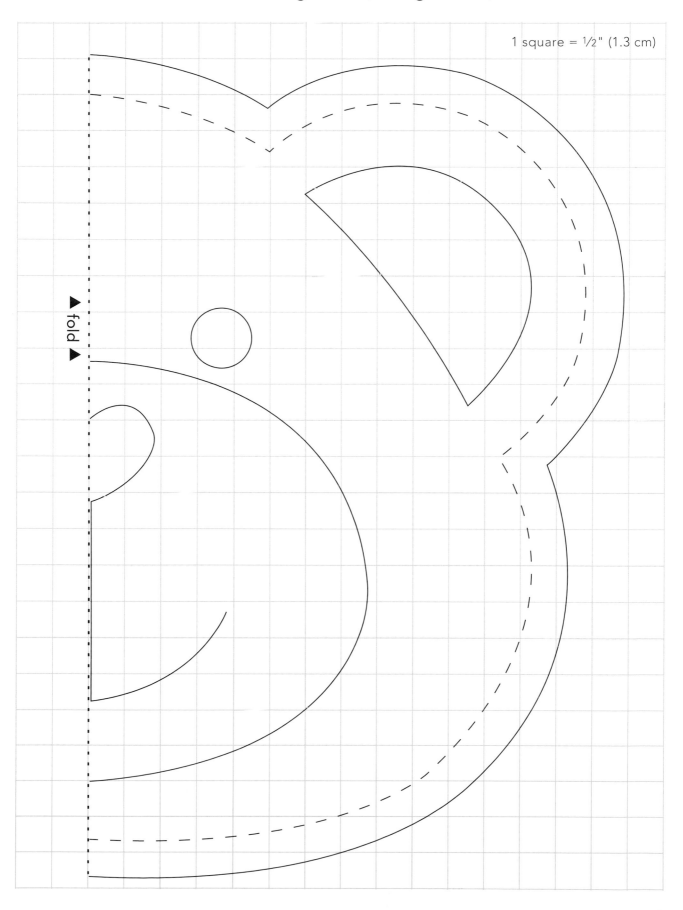

Bearskin Rug Body (enlarge 400%)

1 square = ½" (1.3 cm)

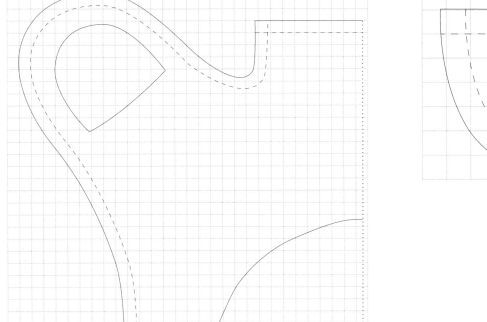

▲ fold ▲

Bearskin Rug Tail (enlarge 200%)

1 square = ½" (1.3 cm)

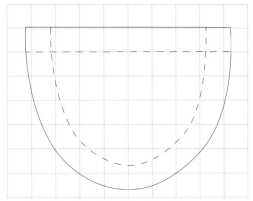

Dinosaur Quilt Body (enlarge to 400%)

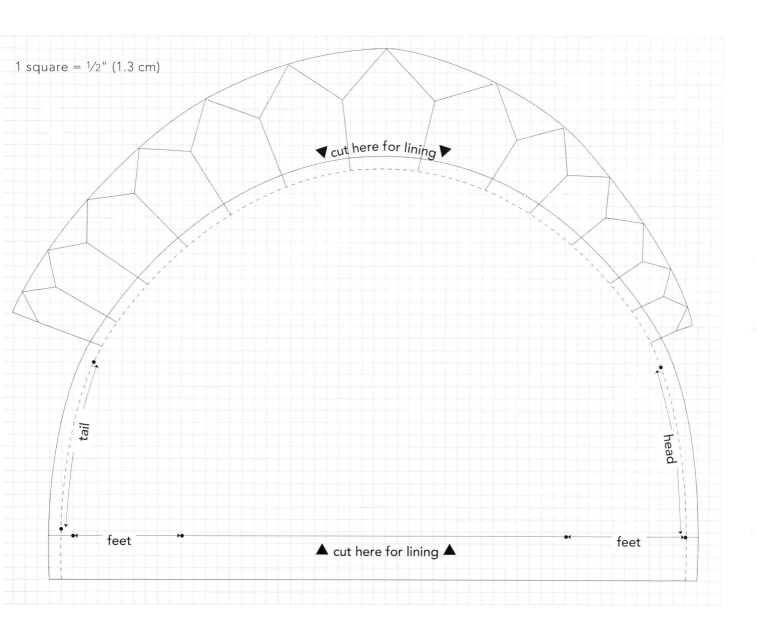

1 square = ½" (1.3 cm)

◀ cut here for lining ▶

tail

head

feet

▲ cut here for lining ▲

feet

Dinosaur Quilt Foot & Spike (enlarge 200%)

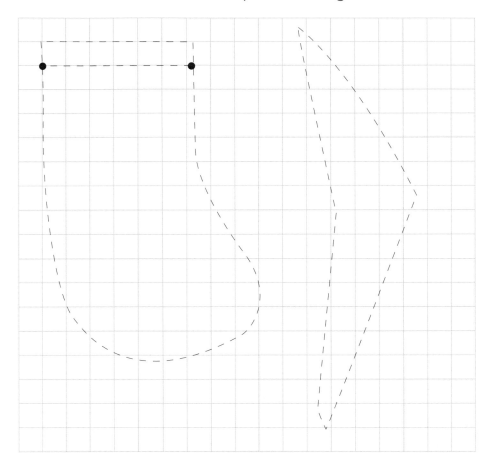

Sunburst Throw (enlarge 200%)

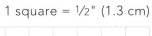

1 square = 1/2" (1.3 cm)

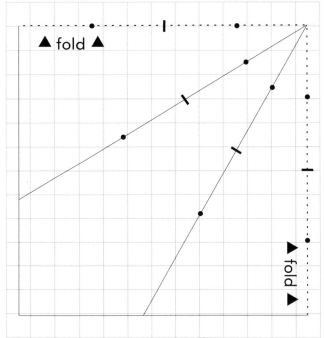

▲ fold ▲

▶ fold ▶

Dinosaur Quilt Head (enlarge 400%)

1 square = ½" (1.3 cm)

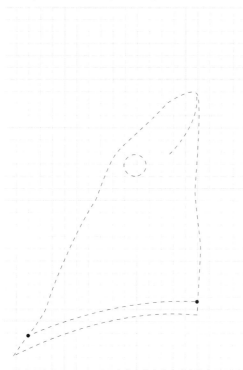

Dinosaur Quilt Tail (enlarge 400%)

1 square = ½" (1.3 cm)

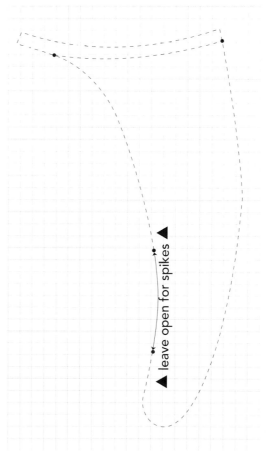

◄ leave open for spikes ◄

Bamboo Tote and Leaf (enlarge 200%)

1 square = ½" (1.3 cm)

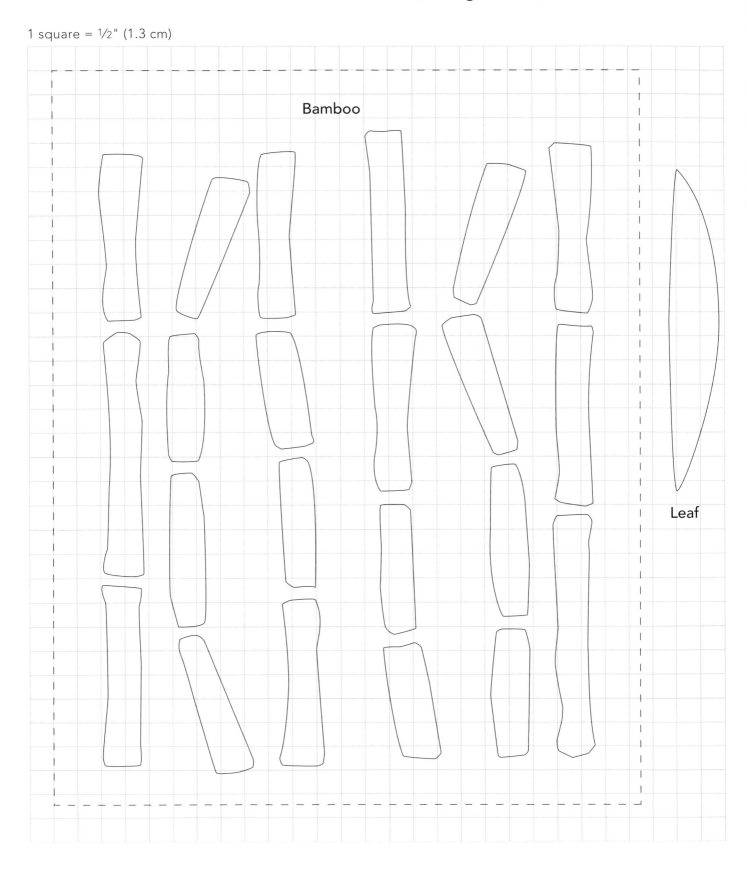

Bamboo

Leaf

Golf Club Covers (enlarge 200%)

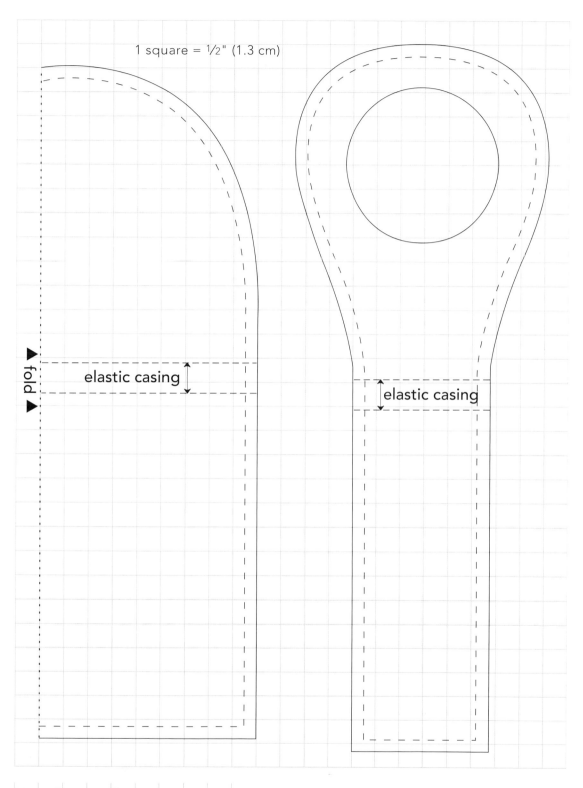

1 square = 1/2" (1.3 cm)

fold

elastic casing

elastic casing

Golf Club Covers Numbers
(enlarge 200%)

1 square = 1/2" (1.3 cm)

Shoveling Mittens (enlarge 200%)

1 square = ½" (1.3 cm)

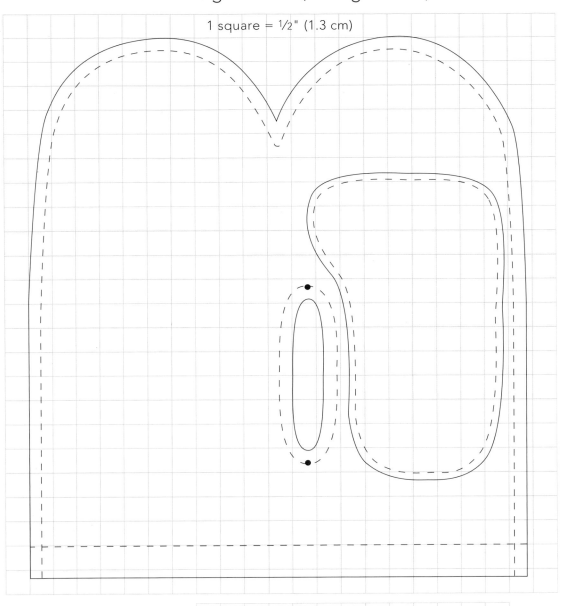

Shoveling
Mittens Thumb
(enlarge 200%)

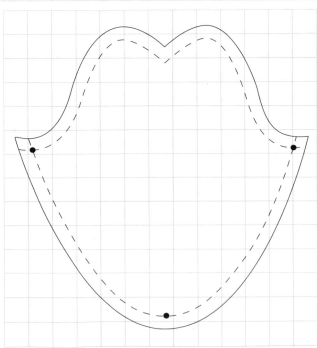